CREATED
Beautiful

SO-AWM-765

Gospel Light

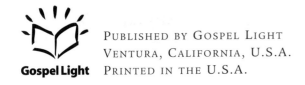

PUBLISHED BY GOSPEL LIGHT
VENTURA, CALIFORNIA, U.S.A.
PRINTED IN THE U.S.A.

Gospel Light is a Christian publisher dedicated to serving the local church. We believe God's vision for Gospel Light is to provide church leaders with biblical, user-friendly materials that will help them evangelize, disciple and minister to children, youth and families.

It is our prayer that this Gospel Light resource will help you discover biblical truth for your own life and help you minister to others. May God richly bless you.

For a free catalog of resources from Gospel Light, please call your Christian supplier or contact us at 1-800-4-GOSPEL *or* www.gospellight.com.

PUBLISHING STAFF
William T. Greig, Chairman · **Dr. Elmer L. Towns,** Senior Consulting Publisher · **Pam Weston,** Editor · **Alex Field,** Acquisition Editor · **Jessie Minassian,** Assistant Editor · **Bayard Taylor, M.Div.,** Senior Editor, Biblical and Theological Issues · **Rosanne Moreland,** Cover and Internal Designer · **Jessie Minassian,** Contributing Writer

ISBN 0-8307-3366-3
© 2005 Focus on the Family
All rights reserved.
Printed in the U.S.A.

contents

Created Beautiful

When God created woman, He instilled in her an indefinable quality that would baffle experts and captivate hearts. Every woman possesses an inexplicable allure *simply by being a woman.*

Who Defines Beauty?

When we discard the definitions of beauty imposed on us by the media, childhood experiences and sin—whether ours or someone else's—we will be able to embrace God's view of our beauty and womanhood.

Internal Beauty

Many of us have a hard time believing that internal beauty is vastly more important than external good looks, but God wants to free us from Satan's lies and open our eyes to the treasure He has placed within us.

A Beautiful Mind

A woman's mind is the first line of defense against Satan's lies. If we can gain control of our thoughts, replacing negativity with God's truth, we will be free to recognize and acknowledge our internal and external beauty.

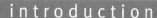

CREATED BEAUTIFUL

Charm is deceptive, and beauty is fleeting;
but a woman who fears the Lord is to be praised.

PROVERBS 31:30

Think back for a moment to the magical world of childhood. When you were three or four years old, were you among the millions of little girls who've dreamed of being princesses when they grew up? Did you ever flaunt your tiny body around the house in a frilly dress and plastic dress-up shoes, waiting for the rest of the world to notice how beautiful you looked? If someone had told you then that you were in fact a beautiful princess, fit for a handsome prince, you wouldn't have argued! You'd have done another pirouette in your dress, then looked up with the most doe-eyed expression you could muster.

If someone were to tell us now that we are beautiful princesses, we'd wonder what they wanted. Somewhere between childhood and adulthood, we lose that blissful confidence. We begin to associate dreaming with disappointment, and as we start to notice all our flaws and compare ourselves with others, we forget the beauty that we possess in God's eyes.

The purpose of this study is to restore the dream that we've lost somewhere along the way. Not that we all need to dress up in frilly dresses and flaunt ourselves, but rather we need to recapture the confidence we once had in ourselves. Because, truthfully, we are no less beautiful today than we were all those years ago. We each possess a unique beauty, and it's time we start living like we believe it.

As you begin this study, ask God to restore a childlike trust that will enable you to believe the promises and the truths you will find in the following pages. Like a child, believe that you are princess material, fit for a loving Prince.

FOCUS ON THE FAMILY'S WOMEN'S MINISTRY SERIES

*And this is my prayer: that your love may abound more and more in knowledge
and depth of insight, so that you may be able to discern what is best and may be pure
and blameless until the day of Christ, filled with the fruit of righteousness that
comes through Jesus Christ—to the glory and praise of God.*

PHILIPPIANS 1:9-11

The goal of this series is to help women identify who they are, based on their unique nature and in the light of God's Word. We hope that each woman who is touched by this series will understand her heavenly Father's unfathomable love for her and that her life has a divine purpose and value. This series also has a secondary goal: That as women pursue their relationship with God, they will also understand the importance of building relationships with other women to enrich their own lives and grow personally, as well as help others understand their God-given worth and purpose.

Session Overview

Created Beautiful can be used in a variety of situations, including small-group Bible studies, Sunday School classes or mentoring relationships. An individual can also use this book as an at-home study tool.

Each session contains four main components.

Everyday Woman

This section introduces the topic for the session by giving you a personal glimpse into the life of an ordinary woman—someone you can relate to—and it asks probing questions to help you focus on the theme of the session.

Eternal Wisdom

This is the Bible study portion in which you will read Scripture and answer questions to help discover lasting truths from God's Word.

Enduring Hope

This section provides questions and commentary that encourage you to place your hope in God's plan.

Everyday Life

This is a time to reflect on ways that the Lord is calling you to change, suggesting steps you can take to get there. It is also a time for the whole group to pray and encourage one another.

Journaling

We encourage you to keep a journal while you are working through this study. A personal journal chronicles your spiritual journey, recording prayers, thoughts and events along the way. Reviewing past journal entries is a faith-building exercise that allows you to see how God has worked in your life—by resolving a situation, changing an attitude, answering your prayers or helping you grow more like Christ.

Leader's Discussion Guide

A leader's discussion guide is included at the end of this book to help leaders encourage participation, lead discussions and develop relationships.

There are additional helps for leading small groups or mentoring relationships in *The Focus on the Family Women's Ministry Guide.*

CREATED
Beautiful

How beautiful you are and how pleasing, O love, with your delights!
SONG OF SONGS 7:6

*Women are beautiful to us because God made them that way. Their beauty and our desire
are God-given. The nakedness of a woman has a powerful impact on us.*
HENRY J. ROGERS, *THE SILENT WAR*

EVERYDAY WOMAN

From an interview with Rhonda, age 33, graphic designer

Q: How would you define beauty?

A: I think beauty is hard to define because it means something different to
everyone. I think someone who is confident, kind and tries to stay
healthy is beautiful. I don't think certain physical traits can define beauty because it is all a matter of opinion.

Q: Do you believe you are beautiful inside and out?

A: Yes. But I don't think I live as healthy a lifestyle as I should. I like my
legs, my behind and my smile, but I still wish I could change certain
things about me—like my curly hair and short torso.

Q: Why do you think women run such a high risk of being unhappy with their bodies?

A: Because society is constantly telling us that we need to look like celebrities to be beautiful. We feel we aren't beautiful until we can look like the images we see on TV.

Q: What advice would you give someone who believes she is worthless or ugly?

A: Write down the positive things you do like about yourself. Pick one or two things that you have the power to change and focus on improving those things (e.g., exercise more or get a new haircut), and then let the rest go. Try to love yourself in spite of your flaws and see them as part of your uniqueness. Plus, remember that Britney Spears and all those other women have people to do their hair and makeup, a personal trainer and chef, and they *still* need to be enhanced by the computer to achieve the look we see. God loves us for us, and we don't have to aspire to look like what we see in the magazines.

According to one research group, the average person sees between 400 and 600 advertisements a day.[1] With all that competition, each company's goal becomes devising the most effective ads to sell their products. To reach their goal, advertising research firms have actually concocted a device that can track a person's visual path, educating companies on the best possible advertising schemes. They have found ways to increase the amount of time a person spends looking at an advertisement by 1, 2, even 3 percent. But one method tops the charts. By including a picture of a beautiful woman, advertisers can increase either a male or female consumer's viewing time by 14 to 30 percent![2]

1. Why do you think a picture of a woman is an advertiser's best friend?

2. In what ways do you think women are inherently beautiful just by being women, regardless of the media's standards of beauty?

To truly see ourselves as beautifully created, let's see what our creator says about us.

ETERNAL WISDOM

Men and women are different.

This is not a big surprise, but have you ever stopped to consider the differences? Apart from the emotional and psychological differences between men and women, our bodies are very different, and we're not just talking about the different equipment you learned about in your junior high sex-education course. Take a look at the following chart that highlights just some of the physical differences between men and women. Fill in the remainder of the chart with your own examples.

Men	Women
Angular features	*Softly curved features*
Rough skin	*Smooth skin*
More body hair; coarser texture	*Less body hair; finer texture*
Upper body muscular strength	*Lower body muscular strength*

When God created woman, He instilled in her an indefinable quality that would baffle experts and captivate hearts. Artists try to replicate it; poets try to explain it and musicians try to win over the women that embody it. Every woman possesses an inexplicable allure *simply by being a woman.*

In Proverbs 5:15-19, Solomon charges men to rejoice in the wife God has blessed them with. He says, "May you ever be *captivated* by her love" (verse 19, *emphasis added*). The Hebrew word translated here as "captivated," *shagah*, appears in other translations as "ravished" (*KJV*), "exhilarated" (*NASB*) and "enraptured" (*NKJV*). But perhaps the closest translation to shagah is "intoxicated" as found in the *English Standard Version.*[3] Shagah implies being led astray or figuratively misled, like a man hopelessly—though perhaps pleasantly—drunk.

3. What does this passage infer about the inherent charm a woman possesses?

   How might an immoral woman use this power to her advantage?

   How could a righteous woman use this power to her advantage in the context of marriage?

Solomon was quite the romantic. Nowhere does his Romeo style shine more explicitly than in the love story in Song of Songs.[4] He understood true beauty, and his descriptions of it may surprise you.

4. In Song of Songs 7:1-9, what aspects of his wife did Solomon find beautiful?

Have you ever considered that your feet, belly button, neck and, yes, even breath (with the proper oral hygiene!) can completely captivate a man? Though Solomon's similes may seem a bit strange to us—"Your nose is like the tower of Lebanon"—his fixation with her body is genuine.

Notice that Solomon didn't point out her particular weight, height, hair type, skin texture or bra size—many of the things with which we women are obsessed. He simply admired his wife's body, and rightly so; being female, she was a wonder to behold.

Of course, being a woman, it wasn't enough for the Shulamite woman to have the admiration of the king of Israel. She still found flaws in her appearance!

5. According to Song of Songs 1:6, of what was the Shulamite woman ashamed?

   How did she get that way?

   How is her insecurity ironic when compared to today's standards of beauty?

6. Which beautiful features of your own body do you regularly overlook and instead focus on those things you wish you could change?

Unfortunately, many of us have lost sight of the mysterious, captivating beauty of our own bodies because we have shifted our focus from God's standard of beauty to society's ever-changing ideal that is only attainable by a minority of women. We'll discuss this inaccessible standard further in session 2. But before we do, let's discuss the hope we have as women designed by the God of the universe.

ENDURING HOPE

Read one man's observation of God's care in the creation of woman.

> The Master Artist who sculpted the universe spared nothing in the creation of this masterpiece. I've asked men on numerous occasions what they think is the most beautiful sight on earth . . . they'll always say, 'A gorgeous woman.'"[5]

7. Do you believe that God spared nothing when creating you, His masterpiece? Why or why not?

Many of us who answered yes to the previous question continue to struggle with self-degrading thoughts and feelings of inadequacy. Why do we have such a difficult time internalizing what we know to be true? Consider one woman's answer to that question.

> A woman can only feel as valued as she respects the person who is valuing her. There have been many guys who asked me out or wanted to get to know me, but I not only wasn't attracted to them, I practically despised them! Their attraction to me made me feel even lower at times! But when a man or woman I trust and hold in high esteem sees me as beautiful and valuable, I begin to believe it more and more. Maybe if we understood how much God values and loves us—and how important His opinion is—it would change how we view ourselves.—Allison, age 24

8. In your estimation, how valuable is God's opinion of you? Explain.

If you were honest with yourself, whose opinion do you hold in higher esteem than God's? A friend's? A man's? Society's? Your own? Explain why.

How has this shift in your focus affected your perceptions of yourself?

9. As you read the following verses, note what each says about God's perceptions of you:

Genesis 1:27,31

1 Samuel 16:7

Psalm 139:13-16

Zephaniah 3:17

1 Corinthians 6:19-20

Most of us know the right answers about how God views us. When asked, most women will say that God made them perfect just the way they are and that they shouldn't care what others think. Yet if those same women were asked, "If it were up to you, would you have made yourself just the way you are?" most—if not all—would say no.

Perhaps if we truly held God's opinion in the highest regard, we would practice the right answers we know so well. There is tremendous hope and freedom in truly believing and embracing God's view of us. Are you willing to do whatever it takes to get there? Before moving on to the next section, talk to God about the way He views you and ask Him for the strength to completely believe Him.

EVERYDAY LIFE

If we are to embrace God's view of us, His masterpieces, we must first know how He views us. Earlier we looked at Psalm 139:13-16, which describes you as "knit together" by God and "wonderfully made" by Him. It's obvious that He planned even the smallest details of your unique design.

On the next page, write a letter from God to you, telling you how much He loves every aspect of the body He created for you. Be specific. Don't ignore those things about you that you would rather change—allow Him to speak to you about the beauty you possess.

Notes

1. Angela Bole, "We Must Stop Glorifying Physical Beauty," *The Minnesota Daily Online*, December 9, 1999. http://www.mndaily.com/daily/1999/12/09/editorial_opinions/o21209/ (accessed October 11, 2004).

2. Dannah Gresh, *Secret Keeper* (Chicago, IL: Moody Press, 2002), p. 19.

3. James Strong, *The New Strong's Expanded Exhaustive Concordance of the Bible* (Nashville, TN: Thomas Nelson, 2001), Hebrew #7686.

4. Although scholars disagree on the allegorical implications of the Song of Songs, this study will focus solely on a literal interpretation.

5. Bill Perkins, *When Good Men Are Tempted* (Grand Rapids: Zondervan Publishing House, 1997), p. 13, as quoted in Dannah Gresh, *Secret Keeper* (Chicago, IL: Moody Press, 2002), pp. 18-19.

Beautiful daughter,

Your loving designer,
God

WHO DEFINES *Beauty?*

The Lord does not look at the things man looks at. Man looks at the outward appearance, but the Lord looks at the heart.

1 SAMUEL 16:7

To emphasize only the beautiful seems to me to be like a mathematical system that only concerns itself with positive numbers.

PAUL KLEE, SWISS PAINTER (1879-1940)

EVERYDAY WOMAN

From an interview with Cassandra, age 21, church ministry consultant

Q: Describe the perfect woman.

A: She would be tall (5'8"), have shiny hair with natural blonde highlights and glowing, naturally tan skin. She would be a size 2 or 4 with curves, and she would have bright, sparkling eyes. Her face—complete with a button nose and a graceful neck and jaw—wouldn't have any blemishes and would be beautiful even without any makeup. Definitely straight, white teeth too! Her breasts would be a size C and she would have a firm bum, long, lean legs and a fit body. Her clothes would be classy and casual but always fresh and always up with the trends.

Q: How does our society's standard of perfection affect the average woman's perception of herself?

A: At one time or another every woman has seen the images of Hollywood and then looked at her body in the mirror and wondered, *Why am I not that beautiful?* or *What do I need to do to look like that?* We think that maybe our husbands or boyfriends would stop looking at other women if we were equally as beautiful, or maybe we wish that we could be respected and admired like they are. So we think, *Maybe if I spend more money on clothes and makeup, bake in the sun for hours and lose weight, I will finally be happy with myself.* I have often struggled with insecurities because I know I can't ever become the woman my brain thinks I should look like. I have battled feelings of defeat, inadequacy, inability to love myself and loathing toward features God has given me. The media's unrealistic portrayal of women is destroying us from the inside out.

In May 2004, a panel of (so-called) experts named Audrey Hepburn the most naturally beautiful woman of all time. On behalf of beverage company Evian, this group of makeup artists, photographers and beauty and fashion editors decided for the rest of humankind that the ideal woman is 5'7", has measurements of 32A-20-35, weighs 110 pounds and wears a size 8 shoe. And, like Audrey, she must have the same measurements from the time she is 23 until the end of her life. So where does that leave the rest of us?

Having a standard of beauty imposed on women is nothing new, but has the standard always been the same? Take a look at this advertisement for Professor Williams's famed Fat-Ten-U Foods from 1891.

> Don't look like the poor unfortunate on the left who tries to cover her poor thin body. Don't suffer from the tortures of inferior devices that artificially fatten with inflationary devices and pads. [Testimonial] In just 4 weeks I gained 39 pounds, a new womanly figure, and much needed fleshiness.[1]

The White Rock mineral water girl is another example of society's changing ideal. In 1959 she was 5'4" and weighed 140 pounds. By the turn of the century she had grown 3 inches, yet amazingly had lost 30 pounds.

Women have been known to do just about anything to be perceived as beautiful. In the Elizabethan age tan skin was out and pale was in. To achieve the look, women would actually ingest small amounts of arsenic! In the 1920s, M. Trielty made his dollar selling M. Trielty's Nose Shaper, described as a "metal object . . . held over the nose by straps buckled around the head and adjusted with screws." Sound over the top? Try imagining how a description of modern-day braces would sound to someone a hundred years ago!

1. How do you think our society's changing standard of ideal beauty has affected women over the centuries?

How does society's ideal affect you personally?

2. On a scale of 1 to 10, how happy are you with the way you look today?

1	2	3	4	5	6	7	8	9	10

I Hate the Way I Look   I Wouldn't Change a Thing

To what extent does your happiness depend on looking like the media's depiction of beauty?

The world's view of beauty is often based on unrealistic standards, and the average woman is left feeling unattractive. But God's Word describes a different standard.

ETERNAL WISDOM

Have you ever stopped and wondered why we call the women who grace TV screens and the covers of magazines *models*? *Webster's Dictionary* defines a "model" as "an example for imitation or emulation."[2] We have model citizens, model homes, model airplanes and role models, but if you're interested in knowing how to be beautiful, well, we have *super*models for that—as if they've attained some higher standard than the rest of us.

God has a model for beauty too, but you won't find it in this month's *Cosmo* or in the latest blockbuster hit. Instead let's turn to 1 Samuel 16. Read the chapter, and then answer the following questions:

3.   What was Samuel looking for in a king?

What does God use to judge whether a person is fit for His service (v. 7)?

Some people have taken this verse to mean that God doesn't care about outward appearances and neither should we. Yet He is the creator of all beauty, and He has given us a desire to create beauty and to be beautiful. In fact, even though God told Samuel not to consider outward appearances when choosing the king, we learn later that Samuel's choice, David, had "a fine appearance and handsome features" (1 Samuel 16:12). Did God contradict Himself?

4. Can God create and love beauty yet be more concerned about what's inside? Explain.

Turn to Ezekiel 28. This passage is a prophecy of judgment against the king of Tyre. Some biblical scholars believe that this passage is also directed at Satan, the ultimate power behind the king. Read Ezekiel 28:11-13,17, and then answer the following questions:

5. What are some words used to describe this king in verses 12-13?

Who was responsible for his perfect beauty?

6. What was the king's downfall, according to verse 17?

How can we become proud on account of our beauty?

God created physical beauty, but He also maintains that there are far more important qualities. He charges us not to focus on physical beauty, or to vainly chase after it, but to humbly embrace what we have been given.

Satan wants to consume us with lies about our bodies—and ultimately about our worth—just as he did the king of Tyre. Satan uses the media to send women blatant and direct lies about beauty, but these are not necessarily the strongest or the most damaging messages we receive.

Women begin developing a perception of their bodies at a very young age and may not even realize from where their present feelings and insecurities come. In the interest of time we can only briefly touch on three areas, but if any of these topics strikes something within you, please seek a respected pastor or Christian counselor to explore these issues further.

> Your pastor may be able to guide you in finding a reputable Christian counselor, or you can call Focus on the Family's counseling department (1-800-A-Family or 1-719-531-3400) for a free consultation by a licensed counselor[3] and a referral to a national counseling service network of more than 2,000 licensed counselors throughout the United States.

Childhood and Early Adolescence

In 2003, *Teen* magazine reported that 35 percent of 6- to 12-year-old girls had been on at least one diet and that 50 to 70 percent of girls with normal weight believed they were overweight.[4] Our perceptions of our bodies are formed at a very young age. In addition to media advertising, peers also affect our perceptions. Teasing remarks such as, "Why is your nose so big?" or "You're as flat as a door!" can scar us for life. Negative comments from family members such as "You're not as pretty as your sister" or "Go change—that dress makes you look fat" can be even more harmful than peer comments, coming from the very people who should love us unconditionally.

7. How has your present body perception been shaped by the comments your peers or family members made when you were young?

Mothers play a critical role in developing a young woman's body image. Mothers who don't teach their daughters how to embrace femininity but instead talk about things like menstruation and sex with shame or embarrassment can be equally—though more subtly—damaging.

8. Did your mother seem confident in who she was as a woman? Did she openly talk to you about womanhood? Explain.

How has her perception of her body affected your perception of your own?

Abuse

Molestation, rape or other sexual abuse often warps a woman's view of her sexuality and sends her spiraling into a cycle of shame, disillusionment and disgust toward her body. She may see her sexuality, and therefore her body, as dirty or as something to be ashamed of.

If you have been sexually abused in any way, we encourage you to seek help from a reputable Christian counselor. God desires to restore your heart and to clothe you in beauty. He wants to replace your shame, guilt and hurt with His comfort and peace.

Pornography

Many women can point to a premature sexual awakening as a child or teenager prompted by pornography that they either stumbled upon or that was forced upon them. Perhaps you can relate to the following story:

When I was about 13, I accidentally got an eyeful of an adult film channel. Only 30 seconds of pornography and my memory was scarred for life. I saw those crude images and subconsciously developed the idea that women are expected to be erotic and sexual if they want the affection of a man.—Cassandra, age 21

Pornography affects all women in conscious and subconscious ways. It degrades a woman's sensuality and strips her of her mystery and dignity. Whether it comes from a magazine, book or movie, those images can burn in our minds longer and with more intensity than any other image.

9. Has pornography affected your perception of your body or your womanhood? Explain.

A prematurely awakened sexuality often leads to masturbation. While masturbation used to be a largely male addiction, more and more women have been caught in this cycle of sexual gratification, heightening their sense of shame, guilt and disillusionment about their bodies. Consider the following story:

I was eight years old when a friend from school introduced me to masturbation. She gave me a children's book designed to teach kids about the birds and the bees and told me to go to one bed and she would go to another until we had both acted out. It was embarrassing, but I was hooked. The overwhelming cycle of shame and remorse continued for 14 years. I never told anyone. I didn't think they would ever look at me the same way again.—Kelly, age 38

Note: For more information on prematurely awakened sexuality and a healthy view of womanhood, we recommend *Kissed the Girls and Made Them Cry: Why Women Lose When They Give In* by Lisa Bevere (Thomas Nelson, 2002).

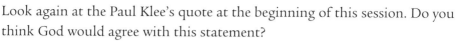

Look again at the Paul Klee's quote at the beginning of this session. Do you think God would agree with this statement?

Klee's quote is similar to an analogy the apostle Paul gave in 1 Corinthians 12. He said that all members of the Body of Christ have equal value, and none of them can exist without the others. Even the "unpresentable" parts are equal. In fact, God has given those parts "special honor." God has arranged each of us to play a specific role in the Body, so who are we to judge one another?

Although the apostle Paul used the analogy to teach the Corinthians about spiritual gifts, the principle of trusting God's divine omniscience can carry over into our view of our bodies as well as others' views of us.

10. Complete the following statement: I am content with my body until I compare it with

11. Place a check mark next to the following statement that most applies to you.

- ❏ When I see a beautiful woman, I tend to point out her flaws to myself or to others.
- ❏ When I see a beautiful woman, I tend to think about how ugly I am compared to her.
- ❏ When I see a beautiful woman, I figure she's probably a mean person and not worth my time.
- ❏ When I see a beautiful woman, it doesn't faze me. We're both women, after all!

Women are notorious for playing the comparison game. Mentally assessing every woman who crosses our path will leave us feeling inferior (or at times, superior), and it steals energy better spent elsewhere. In fact, there is incredible hope, peace and freedom in *not* comparing ourselves to others.

Review your answer to question 11. If you placed a check mark in the first or third box, try focusing on the positive attributes of others. When an average-looking woman walks past you, mentally point out the positive, beautiful things you see in her. Amazingly, as you focus on her beauty, you'll be more apt to appreciate your own.

If you placed a check mark in the second box, focus on your positive attributes and resist the temptation to put yourself down. You can't change anything with a negative attitude, and you might be surprised at how much you can fix with a positive one!

12. If you were to stop comparing your body to those of others, how do you think your perception of yourself would change?

13. Have you ever known a woman who would not be considered beautiful by the world's standards, but who struck you as beautiful nonetheless? What was it about the woman that made you see her beauty?

Our definition of beauty may be marred by the media's or society's distorted view, but we have a loving Father who sees each of His daughters as uniquely beautiful. When we view others through His eyes, we will see beauty where the world doesn't.

When we discard the definitions of beauty imposed on us by the media, childhood experiences and sin (either ours or someone else's), we will be able to embrace God's view of our beauty and womanhood. Before you complete the following activity, spend a few moments in prayer, asking God to lift the oppressive standards you have imposed on yourself and reveal the truly beautiful woman He has created you to be.

Now, in the space provided, draw a picture of your body. Try to make it a fairly accurate depiction of you, but don't feel intimidated if sketching isn't your strong suit! Now go back over the picture and label seven body parts using positive adjectives or descriptive terms (e.g., "cheerful smile," "long legs," "strong body," etc.).

Every time you look in a mirror this week, mentally label your body parts with the positive adjectives in your picture. Don't let yourself focus on the things you would rather change, but instead be liberated by accepting the beauty with which God has blessed you.

Notes

1. Linda Rellergert, "Body Image Advertising," *Missouri Families*, an online publication of the University of Missouri, April 5, 2004. http://missourifamilies.org/features/nutritionarticles/nut43.htm (accessed October 25, 2004).
2. *Merriam-Webster's Collegiate Dictionary*, 11th ed., s.v. "model."
3. Counselors at Focus on the Family are licensed in the state of Colorado.
4. Tom Neven and Rhonda Handlon, "Media Images Affect Teens at Both Extremes," *Plugged In*, August 2004, vol. 9, no. 8, p. 3.

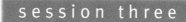
INTERNAL
Beauty

Your beauty should not come from outward adornment, such as braided hair and the wearing
of gold jewelry and fine clothes. Instead, it should be that of your inner self, the unfading
beauty of a gentle and quiet spirit, which is of great worth in God's sight.

1 PETER 3:3-4

A truly beautiful woman makes the best of her physical assets but, more importantly,
she also radiates a personal quality which is attractive.

NANCY BAKER, *THE BEAUTY TRAP*

EVERYDAY WOMAN

From an interview with Rachel, age 46, homemaker, mother, speech/language pathologist

Q: When people say that true beauty is on the inside, do you believe them? Do you believe internal beauty is enough?

A: I must confess that I hear it with some skepticism, primarily due to the immense focus on beauty and youth in our American culture. I have to rest in the assurance of God's Word that to Him my beauty and worth begins in that place where I totally submit my life, my identity and my significance to Him. There is an unfading beauty that comes from a passionate and intimate relationship with Jesus Christ. I believe that there is a place where beauty is birthed in our spirit that brings forth truth.

This truth looks beyond any mirror, fashion magazine or movie star that tries to tell me where I rank on the beauty scale.

Q: How many hours a week do you spend making yourself more beautiful on the outside?

A: I probably spent more time on my appearance when I was younger, fighting acne and finding my personal style. Now that the wrinkles—or, as I affectionately call them, "character lines"—have become more permanent and my muscles have shifted into places I never knew existed, I have focused my efforts on maintaining what I have rather than trying to create something that never was. In total I spend approximately four to five hours a week focused on exercise and beauty.

Q: How do you think a woman's internal beauty or lack of it affects the way people see her external beauty?

A: I'm beginning to see that there is a beauty that comes with maturity, wisdom, unconditional love, commitment to the covenants you have made and most importantly, a passionate intimacy with the Lord. In my opinion, one of the most beautiful women in the world was Mother Teresa. Although she was not pretty by any worldly standard, her devotion to God, commitment to His call on her life, her integrity and the obvious indwelling of Christ in her brought forth an otherworldly beauty. Her humility portrayed strength and a witness that was beautiful by every possible definition of the word.

At one time or another we have all been told some variation of "It's what's inside that counts," "Don't judge a book by its cover" or "Beauty is only skin deep," usually by some well-wisher at a time when we were lamenting that we weren't as pretty as the other girls. For many of us, these simple adages seem like a Band-Aid for a severed limb—these words do little to assuage the insecurities we feel. No matter how many times we hear that external beauty isn't all there is to life, there remains a part of us that doesn't believe a word of it.

1. Why do you think women have such a hard time believing that internal beauty is more important than external beauty?

2. If you were to rate the importance you place on external versus internal beauty, what percentage would you give each category out of 100 percent (e.g., 40 percent external beauty, 60 percent internal beauty)?

Many of us have a hard time believing that internal beauty is vastly more important than external good looks, but God wants to free us from Satan's lies and open our eyes to the treasure He has placed within us.

ETERNAL WISDOM

God has never focused on outward appearances. He is far more concerned with the state of our hearts than with our weight, height or physical appeal. Of course, neither does He shun beauty. As we learned in session 2, God is the creator of beauty and the master designer of our bodies. However, we have become so focused on our external shell that we have neglected the unfading beauty of our internal selves.

3. According to 1 Peter 3:3-4, where does true beauty originate?

Perhaps, like many women, you bristled a bit when you read verse 4. Maybe you thought, *Gentle and quiet? Who does this Paul think he is? It sounds like he's saying that women are weak and don't have anything intelligent to say.* At first glance, some women might consider this verse demeaning to women. But let's look at the true meaning behind the words "gentle" and "quiet."

The Greek word translated as "gentle" in this verse, *praus*, is closely tied with humility and meekness.[1] Meekness has been called power under control. It means having the power to fight back but choosing not to. It means having just cause to resent someone yet choosing to forgive. Praus is a rare grace that has the power to disarm someone on the offense rather than aggravate him or her. There is nothing weak about this quality!

The Greek word translated here as "quiet," *hesuchios*, refers to an inner tranquility.[2] Paul wasn't implying that women should keep their mouths shut or that they don't have anything intelligent to say. Rather, he was encouraging women to develop an inner peace and strength that transcends the busyness—and busybodies—around us.

4. Considering the meanings of the Greek words "praus" and "hesuchios," how might a gentle and quiet spirit enhance a woman's internal beauty?

5. Verse 4 says that a gentle and quiet spirit are "of great worth in God's sight." Why do you think He values these characteristics particularly in women?

What other characteristics do you think are of great worth in God's sight?

The *New King James Version* of verse 3 reads, "Do not let your adornment be *merely* outward" (emphasis added). We aren't prohibited from looking nice, wearing jewelry or doing our hair, but we cannot let those things become our masters. Recall the warning to the king of Tyre we discussed in session 2. God was angry with him not because of his beauty but because of his pride. When we shift our primary focus from God to our clothes, hair, jewelry and other adornments, it becomes sin.

6.   Read the following list. Consider how much time and money you spend on each category. Check the box next to each "outward adornment" that you place too much focus on.

- ❑   Accessories (purses, shoes, etc.)
- ❑   Clothing
- ❑   Hair (cut, color and styling)
- ❑   Jewelry
- ❑   Makeup
- ❑   Nails (hands or feet)
- ❑   Perfume
- ❑   Skin (tanning, facials, etc.)
- ❑   Weight or size

The story of Esther shows us this delicate balance between internal and external beauty. Esther was a complete knockout—stunning enough to win a countrywide beauty contest. Yet it wasn't her outward beauty that changed the course of history.

I must confess that there are days when I dream of having an "Esther Getaway." When I read in Scripture of her year of beauty treatments cloistered away with her handmaidens or friends, it sounds so luxurious and extravagant. What I love about her testimony, though, is that her external beauty may have brought her into the king's presence, but her obedience and reverence to God brought her favor with the king. Esther's prayer life, wisdom, obedience to her call and honor toward those in authority over her brought forth the miraculous. She became a history maker, not because of her beauty, but because she was obedient and arose to God's specific call on her life.—Rachel, age 46

Esther was an example of someone whose external beauty was eclipsed by her internal beauty—a rarity! But what about those of us who would never even *consider* entering a beauty contest?

God made a significant statement when He created the body that would house His divine Son, Jesus Christ. Read Isaiah 53:2-3, a prophecy about Jesus and a description of His outward appearance.

7. Why do you think God chose to give Jesus a body that "had no beauty or majesty"?

Although there was nothing in Jesus' appearance that attracted people to Him, hundreds, even thousands, were drawn to Him—to His teaching, kindness, love, confidence and faith.

8. If God had given Jesus a body like the latest Hollywood superstar, how might His appearance have hindered His ministry?

9. Describe the benefits you can enjoy just because you are you. Consider your internal beauty as well as your external beauty.

Most people are easily intimidated by beauty; but a warm, caring, intelligent person draws us to him or her. It doesn't matter if you're not the next cast member on Baywatch—you can be an average-looking woman with a caring and warm heart who, by not intimidating others, can lead them closer to God.

ENDURING HOPE

Proverbs 31:30 says "Beauty is fleeting; but a woman who fears the LORD is to be praised." It's a verse many of us have heard and have perhaps even memorized. Do you believe it? Your answer to that question may depend on your age. The older we women get, the more we realize that beauty is a bird with wings—and crow's feet are just the beginning!

Once we stop clinging to our physical bodies and embrace our devotion to God, a huge burden is lifted from our shoulders. We no longer have to compare ourselves to the 17-year-old models on magazine covers and can instead embrace our inherent beauty—whether we are 20, 80 or anywhere in between.

10. Have you ever known a woman who soured with age? What do you think caused her bitterness?

Describe an older woman who seems to have sweetened as the years have gone by. What do you think is her secret?

11. How would you like people to describe you in your final years? Will your physical body matter? How about your character and disposition?

What steps must you take in your life today to ensure that those things are said of you?

Just as age improves the flavor of fine wine, the nurturing of our inner selves will make us more beautiful, sweet and desirable as the years pass.

EVERYDAY LIFE

Since we can't change most of the things we dislike about our bodies, it is more productive to focus on the one equalizing factor—that thing that makes plain women shine and beautiful women exquisite: inward beauty. When we focus on cultivating our character, not only will we become more beautiful to others and to God, but also we will be pleasantly surprised as we become more content with our *outside* too.

This week, think about and commit to an "internal beauty treatment." Don't limit yourself to a little eyebrow waxing—this is your opportunity to go for the whole spa experience! Before you decide on what type of inward beauty makeover is right for you, spend time in prayer asking God to reveal areas of your character that need His touch. You can pray the following prayer or your own words:

Father in heaven, You are the most beautiful One in all the universe. You are the author of all earthly beauty, and You have specifically designed me—inside and out—to bring You pleasure. Examine my heart and reveal to me any hidden bitterness, immaturity, sin or other character issue that is marring my beauty. I want to shine so that I can bring You glory and bless others. In Jesus' precious name, amen.

Now it's time to plan your internal beauty treatment. It might include a Bible study for deeper spiritual growth, such as *Experiencing Spiritual Growth* (a Focus on the Family Women's Series Bible study); or it might be a few hours at a park—or even a weekend away—with God, to really focus on the issues in your heart. Use your imagination and listen to what God might be asking you to do. Write your internal beauty treatment ideas in the space provided.

Now do whatever it takes to make time for at least one of these experiences in the near future. If someone offered you a trip to a European spa, you would cancel everything to be there. Treat this experience the same way. Make it a priority—your internal beauty is worth prioritizing and even splurging on!

Notes

1. James Strong, *The New Strong's Expanded Exhaustive Concordance of the Bible* (Nashville, TN: Thomas Nelson, 2001), Greek #4239.
2. Ibid., Greek #2272.

A *Beautiful* MIND

Whatever is true, whatever is noble, whatever is right,
whatever is pure, whatever is lovely, whatever is admirable—
if anything is excellent or praiseworthy—think about such things.
PHILIPPIANS 4:8

When you don't like your body, thoughts and feelings of contempt pour over you. . . .
Most women experience these feelings as mild shame, and they are able to function when
not distracted by occasional negative thoughts and feelings. But others are trapped in
"Bodyhateville" perpetually. They are overcome by guilt, shame, disgust, hopelessness
and anger with each bite of food they put into their mouths. . . . Negative feelings
about your body hinder you from receiving the life God wants for you.
DR. DEBORAH NEWMAN, *LOVING YOUR BODY*

EVERYDAY WOMAN

From an interview with Karen, age 37, interior designer

Q: Have you ever known a woman who couldn't say anything nice about her looks? How did it make you feel? How did it affect your perception of that woman?

A: It seems that in our society it has become a faux pas to say anything negative about another person's body, but it's always fashionable to be negative toward your own. When women I know are negative about their bodies, I feel a kind of adult peer pressure to console them and respond with something negative about myself. It's really too bad because when a friend points out her flaws to me, it only makes me notice her flaws more and think less of her!

Q: Have you ever struggled with negative thoughts about your body? How did you overcome them?

A: I've absolutely struggled with negative thoughts about myself. I don't think I've ever met a woman who hasn't, no matter how beautiful she is. I think the key to overcoming negative thoughts about your body is the same as overcoming any other destructive thoughts—we have to replace Satan's lies with God's truth and choose not to dwell on the negative.

Q: How do you think a woman's negative feelings about herself hinder her from experiencing the life God wants for her?

A: I think God looks down at us and His heart just breaks to see so many beautiful women—that He has created—who can't see past their own noses to recognize just how spectacular they are. If you think about it, we're in essence saying, "I know you're all powerful, God, but I think I could have done better creating me than You did." Anytime we set ourselves higher than God, we're in big trouble! We miss out on the blessings He has for us because we're in rebellion against Him. C. S. Lewis observed that if we would just quit playing in the mud, we would see that God intends us to enjoy a holiday at the sea.

Putting down your body is not pretty. A woman who constantly dwells on her flaws and insists on pointing them out to others might induce sympathy for a time, but she will quickly push others away and make herself miserable.

1. How does hearing women complain about their bodies affect you?

2. On a scale of 1 to 10, how frequently do you make negative comments to others about your body?

1	2	3	4	5	6	7	8	9	10

Never   Sometimes   Often

3. On the same scale, how often do you think negative thoughts about your body?

1	2	3	4	5	6	7	8	9	10

Never   Sometimes   Often

Matthew 12:34 says, "Out of the overflow of the heart the mouth speaks." The negative comments we make about our bodies originate in a heart that has strayed from the truth of God's Word. Some of us don't verbalize our negative thoughts, but that doesn't mean they aren't destroying us on the inside. While not verbalizing these feelings protects others from our negativity, we are still susceptible to self-loathing, eating disorders, depression, chronic dieting and other dangers.

ETERNAL WISDOM

Have you ever listened to yourself think when you're standing in front of a mirror, looking through a magazine filled with beautiful women or trying on clothes? For most of us, these situations bring an onslaught of negative self-talk. Learning to recognize the negative thoughts you have about your body, your worth and the comparisons you make between yourself and other women is vital.

The apostle Peter warned, "Be self-controlled and alert. Your enemy the devil prowls around like a roaring lion looking for someone to devour" (1 Peter 5:8). Satan's influence is not limited to unbelievers. His goal is to get women to doubt what God has said—that we are *truly* beautiful!—and to drown us in a sea of self-pity. He knows that as long as we focus on ourselves, we will be virtually useless to the kingdom of God and, therefore, no longer a threat to him.

If we're going to resist our enemy's attacks, we must first be aware of his tactics.

4. According to 2 Corinthians 11:3, how did Satan deceive Eve?

Satan was able to get Eve to turn away from her "sincere and pure devotion" to God by leading her mind astray. He caused her to question what God had said and tempted her to live independently of Him.

5. Do you question what God says about you? For example, do you question whether God *really* made you beautiful, or do you have a list of things you think God could have done better when He created your body? Explain.

How might Satan use those attitudes to tempt you to live independent of God?

Just as in a physical battle between countries, if you don't understand your enemy's tactics, he will continue to win the spiritual battles he stages against you. We've already seen Satan's battle plan against Eve—according to 2 Corinthians 11:3, he led her mind astray. The Greek word translated "mind" in that verse, *noema*, means "that which thinks, the mind, thoughts or purposes."[1]

6. Second Corinthians 2:11 also uses the word "noema." In this verse, it is translated "schemes." What does that tell you about the nature of Satan's strategy against Christians?

Why does Satan choose this tactic? He knows that our minds are most susceptible to invasive thoughts, so he shoots all sorts of fiery darts at them, aiming where he knows it will hurt most.

7. According to Ephesians 6:13-18, what weapons has God given you to fight Satan's attacks?

Which of these weapons are especially important in helping you stand firm on the battleground of your mind?

Satan knows our weak points, our insecurities and the points which we compare ourselves to the women around us and in the media. Every time we give him an inch, he takes a yard. Remember though that we have God's weapons to help us win the battle for our minds.

ENDURING HOPE

A woman's mind is the first line of defense against Satan's lies. If we can gain control of our thoughts, replacing negativity with God's truth, we will be free to recognize and acknowledge our internal and external beauty.

It is important to identify the bait that Satan uses to tempt you. Before you begin this section, take some time to prepare your heart through prayer.

> *Dear Father,*
>
> *I know that I am your beautiful daughter, and that You want me to live a life free from Satan's lies. Search my mind and reveal any thoughts I harbor about my body that give Satan a foothold in my life, and show me any unhealthy ways in which I subconsciously compare myself to other women. I want to be filled with contentment and with Your Holy Spirit.*
>
> *In Jesus' name, amen.*

Now retreat to a quiet place free from distractions and allow the Lord to reveal the thoughts, attitudes and comparisons to which you are especially susceptible. Record your observations in the spaces provided or in your journal. Some examples have been provided. Use more paper if necessary.

Thoughts I Entertain

- *I hate how big my arms look in short-sleeved shirts.*
- *My nose is huge!*
-
-
-

Attitudes I Have

- *Self-pity*
- *Pride*
-
-
-

Comparisons I Make

- ○ *I compare my breasts with Victoria's Secret models.*
- ○ *I compare my legs with Jennifer's.*
- ○
- ○
- ○

Before you move on, thank God for revealing these areas to you. He may reveal more destructive thoughts, attitudes and comparisons in the days and weeks ahead. When He does, go back and document them in these lists.

EVERYDAY LIFE

It's not enough to recognize the wrong thoughts and attitudes we have about our bodies; we must replace them with truth. As our memory verse Philippians 4:8 teaches, we must choose to think on what is true, noble, right, pure, lovely, admirable, excellent and praiseworthy. You will find these mental guidelines printed below, along with the corresponding Greek words and definitions. Below each definition, write one or two thoughts that combat the wrong thoughts and feelings you recorded on the previous pages. Some examples have been provided.

"Whatever is **true** (*alethes*)"
   Definition: true, truthful, loving the truth, speaking the truth[2]

- ○ *God crafted me with skillful hands and made me beautiful.*
- ○
- ○

"Whatever is **noble** (*semnos*)"
   Definition: venerable, honorable, calling for respect because of character or attainment[3]

- ○ *I deserve honor because I fear the Lord, not because of my measurements.*
- ○
- ○

"Whatever is **right** (*dikaios*)"

Definition: righteous, keeping the commands of God, innocent, guiltless[4]

○ *I choose to focus on developing an internal beauty rather than focusing on an external beauty that fades.*
○
○

"Whatever is **pure** (*hagnos*)"

Definition: pure from carnality, chaste, modest, immaculate, clean[5]

○ *My body is not a sex object but a beautiful vessel to bring glory to God.*
○
○

"Whatever is **lovely** (*prosphiles*)"

Definition: acceptable, pleasing[6]

○ *I like my eyes—they sparkle.*
○
○

"Whatever is **admirable** (*euphemos*)"

Definition: uttering words of good omen, speaking auspiciously[7] (i.e., kindly patronage and guidance)[8]

○ *Mary Ann is a beautiful woman. I think I'll tell her so instead of always feeling like I have to look better than she at Bible study.*
○
○

"If anything is **excellent** (*arete*)"

Definition: a virtuous course of thought, feeling and action; any particular moral excellence, as modesty, purity[9]

○ *I want to dress in a flattering way, but I don't have to dress—or undress—like the models in fashion magazines to be beautiful.*
○
○

"Or **praiseworthy** (*epainos*)"

Definition: praise, commendation[10] (i.e., officially approving of)[11]

O   *I choose to be happy with my body, just the way God has made me.*

O

O

"Think about such things."

Spend this week putting these true thoughts into practice. You'll be surprised how quickly your feelings will follow suit! Dig into God's Word and memorize Scripture verses that specifically combat the lies that Satan feeds you. The more time you spend with God—in His Word and in prayer—the more equipped you will be to take a stand against the lies Satan will tell you about your body and your worth.

Notes

1. James Strong, *The New Strong's Expanded Exhaustive Concordance of the Bible* (Nashville, TN: Thomas Nelson, 2001), Greek #3540.

2. Ibid., Greek #227.

3. Ibid., Greek #4586.

4. Ibid., Greek #1342.

5. Ibid., Greek #53.

6. Ibid., Greek #4375.

7. Ibid., Greek #2163.

8. *Merriam-Webster's Collegiate Dictionary*, 11th ed., s.v. "auspice."

9. Strong, *The New Strong's Expanded Exhaustive Concordance of the Bible*, Greek #703.

10. Ibid., Greek #1868.

11. *Merriam-Webster's Collegiate Dictionary*, s.v. "commend."

Beauty

AND THE Beasts

[Satan] was a murderer from the beginning, not holding to the truth, for there is no truth in him. When he lies, he speaks his native language, for he is a liar and the father of lies.

JOHN 8:44

The greatest deception men suffer is from their own opinions.

LEONARDO DA VINCI

EVERYDAY WOMAN

From an interview with Haley, age 24, publicity coordinator

Q: If you could change three things about your body, what would you change?

A: I think secretly many of us would jump at the chance to be on *Extreme Makeover* and instantly change multiple characteristics about our bodies—from excess fat to the way our toes curl. It's not hard for me to immediately think of three things I would readily change about my appearance. First I would change my hips. I know it's silly, but when I have wanted to look good, I would try to turn to the side to show off my best angle! Then there are my thighs. I inherited the unfortunate thunder-thigh gene from my mother, which, even when I am at my ideal weight, is something to be reckoned with. Third, I wish I had bright and vibrant eyes with long, sultry lashes like the women in the mascara ads.

Q: By changing those things, do you think you'd be completely content with how you look?

A: I think so . . . at first. But as much as I hate to admit it, I know that the fulfillment and joy from those changes would quickly fade. I want to be loved and appreciated for who I am and changing myself to meet a superficial standard won't complete me. Even if I did get my three flaws fixed, I would be so focused on myself that my thoughts, desires and attitudes would overshadow my God-given spirit of joy. Focusing on the wrong things ultimately brings about a sense of worthlessness and depression, no matter how beautiful a person is.

Q: Why do you think we women are so vulnerable to the world's (ultimately Satan's) lies about our beauty and worth?

A: Satan is the ideal advertising and marketing agent! He skillfully encourages us to see our desires as needs, and ultimately lures us with promises that we will be great and likable and everything else we've ever wanted to be. But in reality, to get there we have to dethrone God and put ourselves in His rightful place. I'm guilty of this too, but when we don't take enough time to find our worth in God, we end up looking for quick gratification from the world. But the world can never give us the lasting worth that God wants us to know.

In session 5 we learned that our enemy, Satan, wants to lead us away from our devotion to Christ (see 2 Corinthians 11:3); he'll use whatever means he can get his hands on to do so. We also learned that our minds are where the battles begin.

1. In session 2 we talked about the unrealistic messages women receive from the media. For review, list some of these messages.

2. How do you think Satan uses these lies to lead us away from Christ and to tempt us to live independently of Him?

Satan knows that if he can deceive us into believing that we are ugly, worthless and powerless, we will be practically useless for the kingdom of God.

ETERNAL WISDOM

Satan's lies are like dangerous beasts that threaten to destroy our internal beauty—and mar our view of our external beauty—by undermining our worth and skewing our perceptions of ourselves. Let's spend some time exploring three of these beasts that Satan commonly lets loose against us.

I. My body is who I am and is therefore the most important thing about me.

This beast is a double-headed monster—two lies for the price of one. The first lie is that our bodies define who we are. The second lie is that our physical bodies are the most important things about us.

Let's turn to 1 Corinthians 15:35-49 to find out why this statement is a flat-out lie. Take a few moments to read the passage before moving on.

3. According to this passage, what happens when our physical bodies die (v. 44)?

If we do not cease to exist when our physical bodies die, what can we infer about our true identity?

Our physical bodies are like seeds that will be sown when we die to become heavenly bodies. Our earthly bodies are not all that we are, nor are they the most important things about us. Our salvation and our spiritual health are *much* more important! They ensure that we will receive bodies that will serve us in the heavenly realms.

Look again at verses 39 through 41. Our physical bodies do have a special beauty, just as the moon, sun and animals have unique splendor. God has created vastly different bodies and forms that are suited for all kinds of existence. Have you ever compared your body to the splendor of the stars? The same God made both you and the heavenly lights, each perfectly suited for the existence He has created for you.

II.   I would be completely happy if I were as beautiful as . . .

Insert the name of any movie star, cover model, friend or relative to whom you feel inferior. When we compare ourselves to others, we always come up short. But what if we *could* make ourselves look like someone we admire. Would we be perfectly happy then?

4.   Think back to a time when you *really* wanted something that you eventually did get (a job, car, boyfriend, etc.) Did it solve all your problems? Did it quench every desire, or did you find yourself wanting something else in time? Explain.

Beauty does not ensure happiness. You only need to pick up the latest edition of *People* magazine to see that many of the most beautiful movie stars are extremely discontented people.

5.   According to 1 Timothy 6:6-7, what is "great gain"?

If we can take nothing out of the world (including our physical bodies, clothing and makeup), why should godliness be such an important part of contentment?

Comparing our bodies to those of other women is extremely dangerous. More often than not jealousy, shame, contention and discontentment result when we give in to Satan's lie that we should look like the women around us. Recall from 1 Corinthians 15 that human bodies have their own kind of splendor, different from the splendor of the sun, moon, stars or animals. Part of that splendor is the diversity among people!

III. Anyone can look like a model, and since I don't, I must not be trying hard enough.

Though studies differ, the average American woman is approximately 5'4", weighs 138 pounds with 32 percent body fat and measures 37-29-40. The average model, on the other hand, is between 5'8" and 5'11", weighs 120 pounds with 18 percent body fat and measures 35-24-34. And these numbers still don't factor in differences in skin type, facial features or hair color. The bottom line is that there are many genetic differences among human bodies that make each of us unique from all the others.

Even with a well-balanced diet and regular exercise, chances are you won't be able to look like your favorite supermodel. But the good news is you *aren't meant to!* Rather than look to Hollywood or fashion magazines for your ideal body, it's more realistic to gain your inspiration by looking at the women who share your genetic makeup.

6.   What unique genetic traits—favorable and unfavorable—mark the women in your family?

7. Do you have any female blood relatives who live healthy lifestyles? What do they look like?

Based on your observations, what would be a realistic goal for you to have concerning your body?

No amount of dieting, exercise or plastic surgery can alter your genes. There are certain characteristics you'll have to learn to live with. Some families have a larger-than-average nose. Others have a little extra fat around the abdomen. Still others are shorter than they would like. If you can learn to accept and even appreciate these unique genetic traits, you'll be much more likely to be happy with your internal and external beauty.

ENDURING HOPE

Galatians 5:1 says, "It is for freedom that Christ has set us free. Stand firm, then, and do not let yourselves be burdened again by a yoke of slavery." Though in this passage Paul was specifically addressing the freedom we have in Christ, this principle transcends the context in which we find it. Christ has set us free *so that we can be free!* Yes, it sounds a little obvious, but let's think for a moment about that freedom and what it should mean in our lives.

8. Look up "freedom" in a dictionary and write a short definition below.

9. In the space provided, draw a picture, write a phrase or attach an object that reminds you of true freedom as it relates to embracing your body, mind and spirit.

God has freed us from the beasts that threaten our beauty by giving us victory over Satan and his lies through the death and resurrection of Christ Jesus. However, we must choose to embrace that victory and fight Satan daily, equipped with the armor of God (see Ephesians 6:10-20).

EVERYDAY LIFE

The three lies—or beasts—that we discussed in this session are some of the most common threats to a woman's view of her body image. But there are others, some of which may be very specific to you.

Take a few moments to pray and to reflect on the lies we discussed in this session, as well as the thoughts, attitudes and comparisons you uncovered in the Enduring Hope section of this session.

5. Write down three or four of the beasts with which Satan tries to hound you to undermine your self-worth and your perception of your body.

King David understood the importance of recognizing and verbalizing his emotions, regardless of whether they were rational. In Psalm 73, we can see how David wrestled with the seeming contrast between his observations and feelings and what he knew to be true of God. David's progression through this psalm could be outlined as follows:

1. He felt frustrated and perplexed by what seems unfair.
2. He remembered God's unfailing justice.
3. His feelings fell in line with truth.
4. He proclaimed God's goodness.

Take a moment to read Psalm 73. Now, reflecting on one or more of the lies you wrote above, write your own psalm in the space provided on the next page. Follow the progression of Psalm 73. Incorporate your feelings, no matter how irrational they may seem, until you can get to the place of acknowledging what you know to be true of God and of the beautiful body He has given you.

Ageless BEAUTY

Charm is deceptive, and beauty is fleeting; but a woman who fears the Lord is to be praised.

PROVERBS 31:30

Wrinkles should merely indicate where smiles have been.

MARK TWAIN, *FOLLOWING THE EQUATOR*

EVERYDAY WOMAN

From an interview with Melissa, age 54, homemaker, mother, home health-care specialist

Q: What feelings do you have about your body now that differ from the feelings you had about your body 20 or 30 years ago?

A: Twenty to 30 years ago I always had the hope that I could lose a few pounds to look fit and young. My motivation was to look good—to be appealing and attractive to others. Now my biggest fear is that the weight cannot be lost—that I'm doomed for life! Then I fear that even if I were to lose it, I would still face the problem of so much extra flesh with nothing better to do but hang around—thanks to aging elasticity. Looking good is still a motivation at my age, but as women—yes, myself included—experience more and more physical malfunctions, our motivation to get and stay fit is based more on survival than cosmetic appeal.

Q: Do you think women tend to place more or less emphasis on our bodies and external beauty as we age?

A: I suspect if we worried about our bodies when we were young, we will worry about them as we age. We still place a good amount of emphasis on looking good and feeling great as well. With the myriad aches and pains that keep surfacing, we might appear more aware of how our bodies handle life than how we look living it, but I don't think our desire to be beautiful ever changes.

Q: What do you wish someone had told you when you were younger to prepare you to age gracefully?

A: I wish someone had shared with me how to get myself to listen to and act on all the advice I've heard over the years. Not that I can share the secret with you now, since no one has shared it with me. But if anyone out there has stumbled upon the formula to successfully practice what we hear preached, inquiring minds want to know!

Whether you're 20 or 80 or anywhere in between, there is something you should know—you're only going to get older. Despite humankind's frantic attempts to find the famed fountain of youth, it hasn't successfully concocted any creams, potions, pills, dyes, regimens or surgeries that can stop the aging process. As you may have surmised, not a single mature woman has ever died looking the same way she did when she was born. Aging is a fact of life. And as with most facts of life, you can either embrace it or drive yourself crazy fighting it.

1. How is your body different today from when you were a teenager? Depending on your age and stage in life, how is your body different today from when you got married, had children, turned 40, etc.?

2. Why do you think our society looks down on and tries to hide signs of aging, especially among women?

3. How do you feel about aging? What toll do you expect the process will take on your body? What toll has it already taken on your body?

For some reason society acknowledges that getting older is an inevitable fact of life, yet actually *looking* your age is very last century. Hollywood and the media encourage us to lift, tuck, dye and surgically alter every sign that we're getting older. But to fight the natural processes of aging is unreasonable, and even physically and emotionally dangerous.

ETERNAL WISDOM

They say it happens quite suddenly—even *overnight*. You go about life as usual until one day you look in the mirror and wonder who abducted your young, vibrant body and replaced it with the *old woman* staring back at you. *Is this some sort of a joke?* you wonder. You poke at the fleshiness under your arm, tug at a few grey hairs and using both hands wistfully hoist your breasts a few inches higher. *No, this is definitely not a joke,* you decide. *This is just plain wrong.*

If you can relate to this unsettling scenario, you're not alone. And if this doesn't ring true to you now, just wait a few more years! Every woman reaches a point in time when she is no longer classified among the youthful beauties, but that doesn't mean she ceases to be *beautiful*.

Review our discussion about aging in the Enduring Hope section of session 3 (pages 35-36). When we learn to focus on our internal beauty, aging will only make us more beautiful, sweet and desirable—like a fine wine. Let's look at three keys that will ensure we become *vintage* rather than *vinegary* as the years pass.

Accept the Inevitable

Even if we take paramount care of our bodies, change and deterioration are inevitable. Why? Well, we're all progressing toward an inevitable end: death.

4. Write beside the following references what each passage says about our lives:

Genesis 3:19

Psalm 102:11

Proverbs 31:30

Ecclesiastes 12:1-7

James 4:14

These verses may seem a little pessimistic, but that depends on whether you consider what happens *after* these earthly bodies return to dust!

5. According to 1 Corinthians 15:42-44, what happens to us when our earthly bodies die?

6. How might accepting that your body is going to deteriorate help ease the shock and dismay as the wrinkles come and your body loses some of its tone?

Embrace the Journey

Once we accept that change is inevitable, we can get on with finding and embracing the unique beauty—internal and, yes, even *external*—that comes with each stage of life. The glory of one season of your life differs from the next, but they are each equally valuable.

The following chart divides your life into segments of time. In the second column, describe what changes you experienced or what you expect to experience during that range of time. In the right-hand column, describe at least one unique internal or external characteristic that has or will characterize those years. For example, during the ages of 25 to 39 you may have developed more defined facial features; during the ages of 55 to 69 you may have grown a full head of beautiful, soft silver hair, or you may have taken on a sweeter disposition.

For the segments of time you have not yet reached, project what changes and unique beauty you foresee. You might also ask older women to share what they have found to be true of those seasons.

Ages	Changes That Take Place	Unique Beauty of These Years
0-11		
12-18		
19-24		
25-39		
40-54		
55-69		
70+		

As you think of more changes and unique characteristics throughout the week, come back and record them in your chart. You will enjoy revisiting your predictions years down the road!

Focus on the Blessings

In addition to the unique beauties and characteristics of every age, there are other blessings that come with time. Some of these blessings might include the following:

· A better understanding of yourself
· A deeper relationship with God

- A deeper relationship with your spouse
- Children
- Developed and refined talents
- Financial security
- Grandchildren
- Opportunities for service
- Wisdom

7. Take a moment to reflect on your life thus far. What blessings do you enjoy today that you had not experienced previously in your life?

What blessings do you look forward to?

Focusing on the blessings you have rather than on your aging body will produce more contentment, peace and joy as the years pass. We have nothing to be afraid of and nothing to hide. In fact, we have much to which we can look forward in anticipation!

ENDURING HOPE

Paul often likened our lives as Christians to an athletic competition. You may be familiar with Philippians 3:12-14, in which Paul encouraged his Christian brothers and sisters to keep pressing on until they win the prize of Christlikeness for which they were striving. We are also running that race, and the prize of perfection awaits those of us who stay committed and disciplined until the end—until we die, or until Christ comes back for His Church.

8. To what aspects of perfection are you most looking forward?

A few verses later, Philippians 3:20-21 reads:

> We eagerly await a Savior from [heaven], the Lord Jesus Christ, who, by the power that enables him to bring everything under his control, will transform our lowly bodies so that they will be like his glorious body.

Now there's some perfection! Think about that for a moment—when our earthly bodies pass away, they will become like *Jesus Christ's* body. His body isn't constrained by space and time. That means we will never again have to worry about the effects gravity has on our bodies, or about dimming vision, decaying teeth, thinning hair, varicose veins or flabby arms, thighs and buttocks. And the older we get, *the closer we come to perfection!* So the next time you're tempted to lament a birthday, remember that you're getting closer to your heavenly body, which beats perpetually having 29 candles on your cake any day.

EVERYDAY LIFE

In session 5 we discussed that rather than compare our bodies with those of supermodels, it's more realistic for us to turn to our relatives for inspiration. The same is true as we age. There are some genetic characteristics some women are prone to and others aren't. If your mother, grandmother and aunts developed a slightly pudgy abdomen as they aged, chances are you will too. But on the flip side, there are probably many lovely characteristics— internal and external—that these women developed as they aged.

Take a trip to the attic and dust off some of those forgotten family photo albums. Choose three female blood relatives and gather pictures of them from their youth to old age. Note unique characteristics that the women developed as time passed. Then, in the space provided, list each woman's name and the characteristics that you noticed about her. Include any personality traits that you can remember. **Option:** If you do not have photos of blood relatives or if you do not have contact with any blood relatives, consider any traits you have developed from the influence of those who raised you.

Relative #1:_____

Relative #2:_____

Relative #3:_____

9. Based on your findings, what characteristics—internal and external—will you likely develop as you age?

10. If you listed any unfavorable characteristics, what steps can you take to ensure you will not follow in these women's footsteps?

11. Some have said that you become whom you admire. Think of an older woman who you feel has aged gracefully and who has genuinely become more beautiful with time. Which of her qualities would you like to emulate?

As the years pass, may you come to see the beauty of age and appreciate that gray hair "is a crown of splendor . . . attained by a righteous life" (Proverbs 16:31). And above all, keep your eyes focused on the prize of perfection that awaits all those who put their faith in Christ Jesus.

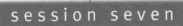

BEASON SEVEN

BEAUTIFUL *You*

Do you not know that your body is a temple of the Holy Spirit,

who is in you, whom you have received from God? You are not your own;

you were bought at a price. Therefore honor God with your body.

1 CORINTHIANS 6:19-20

The real sin against life is to abuse and destroy beauty, even one's own—even more,

one's own, for that has been put in our care and we are responsible for its well-being.

KATHERINE ANN PORTER, SHORT STORY WRITER AND NOVELIST (1890-1980)

EVERYDAY WOMAN

From an interview with Jenna, age 27, secretary

Q: What do you think are the most common ways that women neglect their bodies? How does their neglect affect their body image?

A: Not exercising and not eating properly are the two main ones (guilty!). I think the result of that neglect contributes to a negative body image, especially since we know what we need to do to improve ourselves but may lack the time, energy or motivation to do it.

Q: How much time and energy do you feel a woman should spend improving her looks? When does care become obsession?

A: This is probably different for every woman, but I feel best when I get at least 30 minutes of exercise a day. My morning routine can be squished into 35 minutes, but I feel more improved if I have an hour. I don't think it should be the number one concern of my life, but I have to put a priority on it, or I won't do it. I think it turns into obsession if it becomes your reason for existence, or if your relationships suffer because of it.

Q: What role should exercise play in a woman's life?

A: I know that since I've started exercising again, I feel healthier and more in control of how I look, even though I haven't really seen big results yet. I still know that what I'm doing is going to help me lose the weight that I've put on in the past few years and that helps motivate me to continue. Exercise is weight control as well as personal time that I know is just for me. It's also social; when I exercise with a friend we get to chat—if we can still breathe!

Q: If a woman takes good care of her body, how might that affect her level of happiness with who she is?

A: I know that when I was taking better care of my body, I felt more attractive and more satisfied with who I was. I'm still the same person on the inside, but somehow that doesn't help when you can't fit into your favorite jeans!

We've spent the past six sessions focusing on *not* focusing on our external beauty. Yet none of us can deny the importance of feeling good about our bodies. There is a fine balance here. When we take good care of our bodies, our overall happiness will increase—not to mention feeling healthier. Without altering genes or going through cosmetic surgery, we can increase our level of confidence—and thus become even more *internally* beautiful—just by taking care of the body God has given us.

1. Describe the time in your life when you felt most confident in your body. What specific things were you doing—or not doing—that made you confident?

   Compared with that time, how confident are you now in your body? What do you think has brought about that change?

2. On a scale of 1 to 10, how well do you think you are *presently* taking care of your body?

1	2	3	4	5	6	7	8	9	10

   I Take Better Care of My Car   I'm in Tip-Top Shape

   Whether we know we have room for improvement or we're taking great care of our body, we can always use a little self-evaluation. So let's dig into God's Word and see how we measure up.

ETERNAL WISDOM

After the Israelites escaped from Egypt, God did something completely unthinkable. He—the creator of the entire universe—agreed to regularly meet His people in a physical place. If that wasn't enough, He chose a place made by the hands of men. That's like the president of the United States making regular appearances in a makeshift shantytown in a third-world country—times infinity! Yet within the tabernacle, in the holy of holies, between the two cherubim that covered the seat of the Ark, God personally instructed the high priest on how the Israelites should live (see Exodus 25:22).

3. Read Exodus 40:34-38 for a small glimpse of what it meant for the glory of the Lord to rest on the tabernacle. How is that glory described? How were the Israelites physically able to see it?

Now fast forward nearly 1,500 years where we find God doing the unthinkable yet again. At this point in history, not only did God send His divine Son to dwell among mortal men, He also created an entirely new paradigm for His earthly presence. On the Feast of Shavuot—or Pentecost, as the Greek-speaking Jews called it—which occurred 50 days after the Passover Sabbath (the day that Christ died), God sent His Holy Spirit to indwell all those who believed that Christ was the Messiah.

4. According to Acts 2:1-4, how was this physical manifestation of the Holy Spirit similar to God's indwelling of the tabernacle in Exodus 40? How was it different?

It is significant that God chose to pour out His Holy Spirit on the day of Shavuot. The Jews of Jesus' day celebrated Pentecost in honor of the Torah (or Law) that God gave to Moses on Mount Sinai.

5. Read Jeremiah 31:33 and 2 Corinthians 3:3. Why do you think God might have chosen to send His Holy Spirit to indwell believers on a day dedicated to celebrating the Law He gave to Moses on stone tablets?

6. According to 1 Corinthians 6:19, where has God chosen for His Spirit to now dwell?

For reasons unimaginable to us and in ways we cannot comprehend, God has chosen to make the bodies of believers His modern-day tabernacles. He no longer sits between the cherubim above the Ark to teach the high priest how His people should live. Christ is now our eternal High Priest (see Hebrews 4:14–5:11) and the Holy Spirit personally teaches us how to live. Take a moment to let that sink in!

Look again at 1 Corinthians 6:19, but this time also read verse 20. Because our sinful bodies were not fit for the God of the universe, He had to pay a price to "clean house" before He could live inside us.

7. What price did God pay to make our hearts His home?

Because of the price God paid to redeem our bodies and make them fit for His presence, what are we called to do (v. 20)?

What does the fact that your body is His temple mean to you?

Taking care of our physical bodies seems a small duty in the bigger scheme of things, doesn't it? God chose to pay the ransom for our bodies with the blood of His only Son; then He fills us with His very Spirit who instructs us how to live lives full of peace, love, joy and fulfillment, and all we have to do is *give Him honor* with our bodies. So what does that look like?

8. Review the following list of actions that relate to our bodies. Place a star next to items that honor God. Place an X next to items that don't honor Him. If you're not sure, use a question mark.

_____ Drinking alcohol excessively

_____ Drinking plenty of water

_____ Eating healthily

_____ Exercising regularly

_____ Getting enough rest

_____ Helping others

_____ Maintaining a healthy weight

_____ Smoking

_____ Staying sexually pure[1]

_____ Using good hygiene

_____ Using makeup tastefully

_____ Wearing flattering yet modest clothing

_____ Other:

Now go back over the list and underline the items that you feel you need to work on. Circle the items with which you feel you are doing well.

You probably underlined at least one or two things—but don't be embarrassed if you have many to work on! We're all works in progress. But in light of the marvelous grace that God has extended to us, we owe it to Him to start progressing a little more each day.

Not surprisingly, many women feel the area they most neglect their bodies is their weight. In 2001, 60 percent of the United States population was overweight or obese.[2] Though being overweight is not any worse than other ways we neglect our bodies, it does merit special attention simply because of the sheer number of women who struggle with weight-related issues.

While being overweight is not a sin, putting food in God's rightful place (i.e., turning to food to fill the void that God alone can fill) and gluttony are (see Exodus 20:3; Ezekiel 16:49). While we shouldn't exaggerate these sins, neither can we ignore them. Just like other sins and addictions, if you struggle with maintaining a healthy weight, seek God's help to change. Christ-centered weight-loss programs such as First Place can also help you get back on track. (For more information about the First Place program, visit www.firstplace.org.)

Whether you struggle with weight and/or other hindrances, what keeps you from honoring God with *every* aspect of your body? Place a check mark next to the following root causes:

- ❑ Business
- ❑ Deep emotional pain
- ❑ Feelings of helplessness or hopelessness
- ❑ Lack of self-control
- ❑ Laziness
- ❑ Other:

Honest evaluation is the first step. Choosing to change is the next.

9. What would it take to get your body physically on track with where you feel it should be?

List three specific things you can do to get started.

Before you move on to the next section, spend a few moments in prayer, thanking God for choosing to make your body His temple and asking Him to give you the strength to honor Him with every aspect of it.

ENDURING HOPE

Jenna, our Everyday Woman, made a great point. She said that when she exercises, she feels healthier and more in control of how she looks, even before she sees any results. Though she was talking about weight loss, the same is true of all the different ways we can take care of our bodies. When we choose to honor God with our bodies, He blesses us with greater contentment and confidence in our bodies and in our souls.

10. As you read the following verses, note what each says about the confidence we can have in Christ Jesus:

    Isaiah 32:17

    Ephesians 3:12

    Hebrews 4:16

    Hebrews 10:19-22

We can approach the throne of grace with confidence and ask for "grace to help us in our time of need" (Hebrews 4:16). That includes our need to honor Him with our bodies! He knows that we can't do it in our own strength, and He longs for us to simply acknowledge our lack and ask for His bounty.

The confidence we have in Christ to approach God's throne transcends anything we can do. Yet as we strive to honor God with our bodies, we will naturally become more content and confident, no matter what unchangeable features remain. Now that's something for which to be hopeful!

EVERYDAY LIFE

As was mentioned earlier, honest evaluation is the first step toward becoming a better steward of your body. Complete the following chart. In the left-hand column, write down the items you highlighted from our exercise on page 71. In the middle column, describe how you feel about that area. In the right-hand column, write down two or three specific steps you can implement in the next week to begin honoring God in that area. Use more paper if necessary. An example has been given to get you started.

Area of Neglect	How I Feel About This Area	What I'll Do to Change
Exercising Regularly	*I used to have a regular routine, but I've been so busy lately that I just haven't made the time.*	*1. Walk 1 hour on Saturday* *2. Ask Molly if she wants to start jogging with me twice a week*

After you implement these changes this week, set one-month, six-month and one-year goals. As you begin to see internal and external results, you will find it easier and easier to keep up the good work. However, don't become so focused on the external aspects of your beauty that you neglect the internal beauty that you've discovered these past six sessions.

As we close this study, spend several minutes in prayer, thanking God for all He has taught you about your body, your beauty and your worth in Him. Write your prayer in the space provided on the next page or in your journal.

You are a beautiful creation, designed to bring honor and satisfaction to our creator God! Believe it, embrace it and find your confidence in Him.

Notes

1. Sexual purity is important for both married and single women. While single women are called to purity and to abstain from sex before marriage (see 1 Thessalonians 4:3), married women are also called to sexual purity by keeping the marriage bed undefiled (see Hebrews 13:4).
2. Community Memorial Hospital, *A Community of Caring*, vol. ix, no. 2., p. 5.

CREATED
Beautiful

General Guidelines

1. Your role as a facilitator is to get women talking and discussing areas in their lives that are hindering them in their spiritual growth and personal identity.

2. Be mindful of the time. There are four sections in each study. Don't spend too much time on one section unless it is obvious that God is working in people's lives at a particular moment.

3. Emphasize that the group meeting is a time to encourage and share with one another. Stress the importance of confidentiality—what is shared stays within the group.

4. Fellowship time is very important in building small-group relationships. Providing beverages and light refreshments either before or after each session will encourage a time of informal fellowship.

5. Encourage journaling, as it helps women apply what they are learning and stay focused during personal devotional time.

6. Most women lead very busy lives; respect group members by beginning and ending meetings on time.

7. Always begin and end the meetings with prayer. If your group is small, have the whole group pray together. If it is larger than 10 members, form groups of 2 to 4 to share and pray for one another.

   One suggestion is to assign prayer partners each week. Encourage each group member to complete a Prayer Request Form as she arrives. Members can select a prayer request before leaving the meeting and pray for that person during the week. Or two women can trade prayer requests and then pray for each other at the end of the meeting and throughout the week. Encourage the women to call their prayer partner at least once during the week.

8. Another highly valuable activity is to encourage the women to memorize the key verse each week.

9. Be prepared. Pray for your preparation and for the group members during the week. Don't let one person dominate the discussion. Ask God to help you draw out the quiet ones without putting them on the spot.

10. Enlist the help of other group members to provide refreshments, to greet the women, to lead a discussion group or to call absentees to encourage them, etc. Whatever you can do to involve the women will help bring them back each week.

11. Spend time each meeting worshiping God. This can be done either at the beginning or the end of the meeting.

How to Use the Material

Suggestions for Group Study

There are many ways that this study can be used in a group situation. The most common way is a small-group Bible study format. However, it can also be used in a women's Sunday School class. However you choose to use it, here are some general guidelines to follow for group study:

· Keep the group small—8 to 12 participants is probably the maximum for effective ministry, relationship building and discussion. If you have a larger group, form smaller groups for the discussion time, selecting a facilitator for each group.

· Ask the women to commit to regular attendance for the seven weeks of the study. Regular attendance is a key to building relationships and trust in a group.

· Whatever is discussed in the group meetings is to be held in strictest confidence among group members only.

Suggestions for Mentoring Relationships

This study also lends itself for use in relationships in which one woman mentors another woman. Women in particular are admonished in Scripture to train other women (see Titus 2:3-5).

- A mentoring relationship could be arranged through a system set up by a church or women's ministry.
- A less formal way to start a mentoring relationship is for a younger woman or new believer to take the initiative and approach an older or more spiritually mature woman who exemplifies the Christlike life and ask to meet with her on a regular basis. Or the reverse might be a more mature woman who approaches a younger woman or new believer to begin a mentoring relationship.
- When asked to mentor, someone might shy away, thinking that she could never do that because her own walk with the Lord is less than perfect. But just as we are commanded to disciple new believers, we must learn to disciple others to strengthen their walk. The Lord has promised to be "with you always" (Matthew 28:20).
- When you agree to mentor another woman, be prepared to learn as much or more than the woman you will mentor. You will both be blessed by the mentoring relationship built on the relationship you have together in the Lord.

There are additional helps for mentoring relationships or leading small groups in *The Focus on the Family Women's Ministry Guide*.

SESSION ONE
CREATED BEAUTIFUL

Before the Meeting
The following preparations should be made before each meeting:

1. Gather materials for making name tags (if women do not already know each other and/or if you do not already know everyone's name). Also

gather extra pens or pencils and Bibles to loan to anyone who may need them.

2. Make photocopies of the Prayer Request Form (available in *The Focus on the Family Women's Ministry Guide*, chapter 9), or provide 3x5-inch index cards for recording requests.

3. Read through your own answers and mark the questions that you especially want to have the group discuss.

4. Make the necessary preparations for the ice-breaker activity you choose.

5. Have a white board or poster board and the appropriate felt-tip pens available for the teaching time.

Ice Breakers

1. Distribute Prayer Request Forms, or index cards, and ask each woman to at least write down her name, even if she doesn't have a specific prayer request. This way, someone can pray for her during the upcoming week. This can be done each week. Just because we don't have a specific prayer request doesn't mean we don't need prayer!

2. **Option 1**—Introduce yourself and then share one thing that you think is beautiful about the woman to your right. Go around the circle until all the women have introduced themselves.

   Option 2—For a fun alternative, give each woman a piece of paper and a pen or pencil as she enters the meeting room. When everyone has been seated, instruct the women to put the paper on top of their heads and draw a picture of themselves. Have the women share their pictures with the whole group.

3. Welcome the women and thank them for coming. Begin with prayer for the group and for the study topic.

Discussion

1. **Everyday Woman**—Before the meeting, gather several magazine ads, newspaper ads and/or commercials (recorded onto a VHS tape) that use the female body to increase sales. Discuss each ad or commercial as a group, focusing on the correlation between the product and the woman (or lack thereof). Ask, **Why might a picture of a woman not only cause a man to look longer, but also another woman?** Have volunteers share their answers to question 2.

2. **Eternal Wisdom**—On a piece of poster board or on a white board, recreate the chart on page 10, leaving lots of extra boxes for the women's ideas. Go around the room, invite volunteers to share one physical difference between men and women. Briefly discuss some emotional differences. Discuss: **How do a woman's unique emotional traits add to her allure?** Ask several volunteers to share their answers to questions 3, 5 and 6. Guide the discussion and share your own answers when appropriate, but allow the other women to discuss first.

3. **Enduring Hope**—One of the greatest challenges women face in the area of body image is internalizing what they know to be true. Many of the women will know the right answers but not put the truth into practice, so encourage vulnerability and honesty. You can help by being candid with your own struggles. Form groups of three or four women each to discuss questions 7 through 9, and then come together as a large group for the next section.

4. **Everyday Life**—Invite two or three women to share the prayer they wrote in this section with the rest of the group. Be sensitive to those who would rather not share, as this letter is very personal in nature. Begin by sharing your letter if appropriate. If no one feels comfortable sharing, or if you have extra time, read Psalm 139:13-16 aloud and then discuss how God views those parts of us that we would rather change.

5. **Close in Prayer**—Invite a volunteer to close in prayer, thanking God for the intricate way He has designed each one of you, and asking that you would each be able to embrace your beauty as women. Have each woman exchange her prayer request with another woman. Encourage them to pray for their partner throughout the week.

6. **Encourage Scripture Memory**—Encourage the women to memorize next week's key verse or another verse from the lesson that was especially helpful for them.

After the Meeting

1. **Evaluate**—Spend time evaluating the meeting's effectiveness (see *The Focus on the Family Women's Ministry Guide*, chapter 10, for an evaluation form).

2. **Encourage**—During the week, try to contact each woman (through phone calls, notes of encouragement, e-mails or instant messages) and

welcome her to the study. Make yourself available to answer any questions or concerns the women may have and generally get to know them. If you have a large group, enlist the aid of some women in the group to contact others.

3. **Equip**—Complete the Bible study.

4. **Pray**—Prayerfully prepare for the next meeting, praying for each woman and your own preparation. Discuss with the Lord any apprehension, excitement or anything else that is on your mind regarding the Bible study material or the group members. If you feel inadequate or unprepared, ask for strength and insight. If you feel tired or burdened, ask for God's light yoke. Whatever it is you need, ask God for it. He will provide!

SESSION TWO
WHO DEFINES BEAUTY?

Before the Meeting

1. Make the usual preparations as listed on pages 79-80.
2. Make the necessary preparations for the ice-breaker activity.
3. Gather the necessary materials for the teaching time.

Ice Breakers

1. Distribute Prayer Request Forms, or index cards, and remind women to write down their names, even if they don't have any specific requests this week.
2. As a group, recite the memory verse together.
3. **Before the meeting**, gather several magazines, advertisements and catalogs that contain various pictures of women. You will also need a few pieces of poster board, tape and several pairs of scissors.

   As the women arrive, ask them to cut out as many pictures of women as they can find and then tape them to the pieces of poster board. Allow about 5 to 10 minutes. When the time is up, spend time assessing the subtle and blatant messages these ads and pictures send women. Discuss the effects these messages have on a woman's view of her body and self-worth.

Discussion

1. **Everyday Woman**—Ask the women if they agree with Cassandra's description of the perfect woman. Discuss: **Where do you think her standard comes from?** Invite volunteers to share how the media's depiction of beauty has affected their body image (question 1).

2. **Eternal Wisdom**—Discuss: **Why do people generally look for a standard to follow or to measure ourselves against?** In what other areas beside physical looks do we compare ourselves to others?

    Discuss questions 4 through 6. Be open to address the women's questions, but do not let the conversation become a debate on the identity of the king of Tyre—that is not the point of the lesson! Focus on the dangers of allowing pride or beauty to control us. Review the sections labeled "Childhood and Early Adolescence," "Abuse" and "Pornography." If you sense the women have further questions or need to talk about these issues, spend as much time as needed here. If you do not feel qualified to address an issue raised, direct that woman to someone who can help her with her particular need.

3. **Enduring Hope**—Form groups of three to four to discuss the opening quote and questions 10 through 13. Encourage the women to be honest with themselves and with each other.

4. **Everyday Life**—Still in small groups, have the women share some of the positive adjectives they used to describe their bodies, as well as how they felt when they mentally repeated those terms throughout the week.

5. **Close in Prayer**—With the whole group, join hands and make a large circle. Have each woman pray a short prayer thanking God for the body He has given her. Close the prayer time by asking God to help each of you redefine your standard of beauty based on that of your Creator's. Collect the prayer request forms and have each woman select one to pray for during the week.

    Optional: Invite women who need prayer or counseling to stay after the meeting.

After the Meeting

1. **Evaluate.**
2. **Encourage.** Call the women to encourage them to pray for their prayer partner.
3. **Equip.**
4. **Pray.**

SESSION THREE
INTERNAL BEAUTY

Before the Meeting

1. Make the usual preparations as listed on pages 79-80.
2. Make the necessary preparations for the ice-breaker activity option you choose.

Ice Breakers

1. Distribute Prayer Request Forms, or index cards, and encourage the women to write their names on the forms even if they don't have any specific requests this week. Encourage them to be specific about their requests.
2. Invite volunteers to recite the memory verse, or recite it as a group.
3. **Option 1**: Invite a guest speaker to briefly (approximately 10 minutes) share with your group about the value of internal beauty, an anecdote about trying to look good for others or a short story or poem about internal beauty. Some speaker ideas include a pastor's wife, a disabled or physically impaired woman or anyone whom you feel the women in your group would benefit from hearing.
4. **Option 2**: Invite volunteers to discuss the questions, **When people say that true beauty is on the inside, do you believe them? Do you believe internal beauty is enough?** Encourage the women to be honest and vulnerable.

Discussion

1. **Everyday Woman**—Discuss question 1.
2. **Eternal Wisdom**—Discuss the meanings of *praus* (gentle) and *hesuchios* (quiet). Address any misconceptions the women have about these words or about 1 Peter 3:4. Form groups of three to four to discuss questions 4 through 8.
3. **Enduring Hope**—Still in small groups, ask women to share their answers to 11.
4. **Everyday Life**—As a large group, ask volunteers to share what they did (or plan to do) for their internal beauty treatment. Have as many volunteers share as the time will allow.
5. **Close in Prayer**—Close the group in prayer, thanking God that He does not look at the things that man looks at, but cares more about our hearts. Have the women select a prayer request card from a basket in which you have collected them. Encourage the women to call their prayer partner during the week to pray together over the phone.

    Optional: Invite women who need prayer or counseling to stay after the meeting.
6. **Encourage Scripture Memory**—Encourage the women to memorize next week's key verse or a verse from the lesson that was especially helpful for them.

After the Meeting

1. **Evaluate.**
2. **Encourage.**
3. **Equip.**
4. **Pray.**

A BEAUTIFUL MIND

Before the Meeting

1. Make the usual preparations as listed on pages 79-80.
2. Make the necessary preparations for the ice-breaker activity.
3. Have a white board and/or poster board and the appropriate felt-tip pens available for the teaching time.

Ice Breakers

1. Distribute Prayer Request Forms, or index cards, and encourage the women to write their names on the forms even if they don't have any specific requests this week. Encourage them to be specific about their requests.
2. Instead of a typical ice-breaker activity, serve tea and/or snacks and allow the women a few extra minutes to mingle. Encourage them to talk about issues relating to body image and what they've been learning, but don't be dogmatic. Consider this a time for building the relationships that women need.
3. Invite volunteers to recite the memory verse, or recite it as a group.

Discussion

1. **Everyday Woman**—Ask women to share what they feel are the most common negative comments and thoughts women say and think about their bodies. Record the group's observations on a piece of poster board or on a white board.
2. **Eternal Wisdom**—Discuss how Satan tries to use our thoughts to tempt us to live independently of God. Read Ephesians 6:13-18 aloud, then discuss how each of these weapons relates to our fight against negative thoughts about our body images.
3. **Enduring Hope**—Form groups of three to four to discuss the thoughts, attitudes and comparisons the women listed on pages 43-44.

4. **Everyday Life**—Still in small groups, have the women take turns sharing the thoughts they recorded under each section of Philippians 4:8. Then as a whole group, brainstorm ways that the women can apply these thoughts to their lives.

5. **Close in Prayer**—Ask a volunteer to close the group in prayer, asking God for the strength to stand against Satan's attacks and to think on what is true, noble, right, pure, lovely, admirable, excellent and praiseworthy. Remind women to take a prayer request card as they leave.

   Optional: Invite women who need prayer or counseling to stay after the meeting.

6. **Encourage Scripture Memory**—Encourage the women to memorize next week's key verse or a verse from the lesson that was especially helpful for them.

After the Meeting

1. **Evaluate.**
2. **Encourage.**
3. **Equip.**
4. **Pray.**

SESSION FIVE
BEAUTY AND THE BEASTS

Before the Meeting

1. Make the usual preparations as listed on pages 79-80.
2. Make the necessary preparations for the ice-breaker activity.
3. Have a white board and/or poster board and the appropriate felt-tip pens available for the teaching time.

Ice Breakers

1. Distribute Prayer Request Forms, or index cards, and encourage the women to write their names on the forms even if they don't have any specific requests this week. Encourage them to be specific about their requests.
2. Invite volunteers to recite the memory verse, or recite it as a group.
3. Ask women to share why they think women are so vulnerable to the world's (ultimately Satan's) lies about our beauty and worth. Discuss Haley's answer in the Everyday Women section.

Discussion

1. **Everyday Woman**—Discuss questions 1 and 2 as a group.
2. **Eternal Wisdom**—Review each of the three lies discussed in this section. As you touch on each one, Discuss questions 3 through 7.
3. **Enduring Hope**—Invite volunteers to share what they wrote or drew for question 9. Discuss the freedom that Christ has given us through His victory over death and sin.
4. **Everyday Life**—Invite volunteers to share the psalm they wrote about their feelings toward their bodies and what they know to be true of God. Be prepared to share your own psalm to get things started.
5. **Close in Prayer**—Thank God for giving us the victory over the beasts with which Satan attacks us. Then have each woman pray a sentence thanking God for the body He has given her, for His love or for the victory she has in Christ. Remind women to take a prayer request card before they leave.

    Optional: Invite women who need prayer or counseling to stay after the meeting.
6. **Encourage Scripture Memory**—Encourage the women to memorize next week's key verse or a verse from the lesson that was especially helpful for them.

After the Meeting

1. **Evaluate.**
2. **Encourage.** As you call the women this week, ask them to bring a photo of at least one female relative and be prepared to share with the group at least one beautiful characteristic of that woman.
3. **Equip.**
4. **Pray.**

SESSION SIX
AGELESS BEAUTY

Before the Meeting

1. Make the usual preparations as listed on pages 79-80.
2. Make the necessary preparations for the ice-breaker activity.
3. Have a white board and/or poster board and the appropriate felt-tip pens available for the teaching time.

Ice Breakers

1. Distribute Prayer Request Forms, or index cards, and encourage the women to write their names on the forms even if they don't have any specific requests this week. Encourage them to be specific about their requests.
2. Invite volunteers to recite the memory verse, or recite it as a group.
3. **Before the meeting**, ask each woman to bring a picture of one of the relatives she chose for the Everyday Life section of this session. Have each woman share her picture with the group, pointing out at least one beautiful characteristic—internal or external—that the woman developed as she aged.

Discussion

1. **Everyday Woman**—Ask the women to share one piece of advice about aging gracefully that older women have given them, that they wish they

had heard when they were younger, or that they would like to pass on to younger women now. Record these pieces of advice on a piece of poster board or on a white board.

Option: Ask for a volunteer to compile the pieces of advice and photocopy them to distribute at the next meeting.

2. **Eternal Wisdom**—Review the chart under the "Embrace the Journey" section. Ask volunteers to give their answers for one of the age categories until all the stages have been discussed. (**Option**: Record their answers on a large poster board copy of the chart.)

   On a white board or poster board, record the blessings the women recorded in question 7.

3. **Enduring Hope**— Read Philippians 3:20-21 aloud. Invite volunteers to share the things that they are most looking forward to saying good-bye to when we reach perfection (question 8).

4. **Everyday Life**—Ask volunteers to share what they learned about themselves by completing this section. Discuss: **What do you plan to do to ensure that you inherit the favorable (rather than unfavorable) traits of your relatives?** Ask women to share what they feel they should do if one or more of those traits is inevitable (i.e., unchangeable physical features).

5. **Close in Prayer**—Thank God for the blessings He gives us that only come with age. Then have each woman pray a short prayer asking God to help her to become sweeter and more desirable as the years pass.

   Optional: Invite women who need prayer or counseling to stay after the meeting.

6. **Encourage Scripture Memory**—Encourage the women to memorize next week's key verse or a verse from the lesson that was especially helpful for them.

After the Meeting

1. **Evaluate.**
2. **Encourage.**
3. **Equip.**
4. **Pray.**

BEAUTIFUL YOU

Before the Meeting

1. Make the usual preparations as listed on pages 79-80.
2. Make photocopies of the Study Evaluation Form (see *The Focus on the Family Women's Ministry Guide*, chapter 9).
2. Make the necessary preparations for the ice-breaker activity.

Ice Breakers

1. Distribute Prayer Request Forms, or index cards, and encourage the women to write their names on the forms even if they don't have any specific requests this week. Encourage them to be specific about their requests.
2. Invite volunteers to recite the memory verse, or recite it as a group. Have a special prize for any woman who can say all seven memory verses. (If most of the women have memorized all seven, have the women recite the verses in pairs.)
3. **Option 1**—Invite a beautician, nutritionist, manicurist, personal trainer or other specialist to give a brief presentation on one or more ways that women can take care of their bodies.
    Option 2—Invite volunteers to briefly share one or two things that God has specifically taught them through this study.

Discussion

1. **Everyday Woman**—Discuss whether they agree with Jenna's comments regarding how much time we should spend on our looks each day, how taking care of our bodies affects how we feel about them and what role exercise should play in a woman's life. Discuss: **How can having a greater confidence in our bodies actually deepen our internal beauty?**
2. **Eternal Wisdom**—Review the shift God made from dwelling in the tabernacle to dwelling in human hearts, then form groups of three to four

to discuss the lists on pages 71-72 regarding our actions and what keeps us from honoring God with our bodies. Also discuss question 9.

Be sensitive to women in the group who struggle to maintain a healthy weight. Do not treat being overweight any differently than you would the other areas of neglect—in other words, don't ignore it and don't overemphasize it. If the majority of the women in your group struggle with their weight, you may suggest adding accountability in this area to your regular Bible study meetings.

3. **Enduring Hope**—Invite volunteers to read aloud the verses listed in question 10. Then after sharing their answers, discuss the magnitude of being able to approach God with confidence. Help the women in your group grasp the amazing promises found in these verses!

4. **Everyday Life**—If there is time, ask each woman to share at least one item she included in her chart. Encourage women to share at least enough that they can be held accountable the next time you meet.

5. **Close in Prayer**—Ask each woman to pray a short sentence prayer, thanking God for what He has taught her through the course of this study. When everyone is finished, close the time of prayer, thanking God for what He has taught you and for hand-picking each of the women present to complete the study.

   Optional: Invite women who need prayer or counseling to stay after the meeting.

After the Meeting

1. **Evaluate**—Distribute the Study Evaluation Forms for members to take home with them. Share about the importance of feedback, and ask members to take the time this week to write their review of the group meetings and then return them to you.

2. **Encourage**—Contact each woman during the week to invite her to the next Focus on the Family Women's Bible study.

We've Combined the Best of Women's Ministry for One Comprehensive Experience!

Our aim? Bring women closer to the Lord while helping them build deep, Christ-centered relationships.

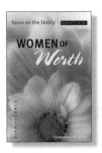

Women of Worth Bible Study
Women often define themselves by what others expect of them. This study helps women find their true identity and purpose through their relationship with Christ.
ISBN 08307.33361

Healing the Heart Bible Study
This study helps women experience emotional and spiritual healing by understanding the hurts and pain in their lives and finding restoration through Christ.
ISBN 08307.33620

Balanced Living Bible Study
When women strive to do it all, they end up feeling stressed out, fatigued and disconnected from God. This study gives women the tools to balance the various demands on their time while maintaining an intimate relationship with God.
ISBN 08307.33639

The Blessings of Friendships Bible Study
In today's fast-paced, busy world it's difficult for women to establish and maintain strong, healthy relationships. In this study, women will explore the nature of relationships and Christ's model for them.
ISBN 08307.33647

Experiencing Spiritual Growth Bible Study
This study is for women who want to nurture a deeper relationship with God and cultivate the fruit of the Spirit described in Galatians 5:22-23. Committing to the spiritual disciplines will result in strong testaments to the grace and glory of God.
ISBN 08307.33655

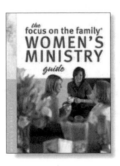

The Focus on the Family Women's Ministry Guide
This comprehensive guide gives leaders everything they need to set up and run an effective ministry for women of all ages and life situations.
ISBN 08307.33388

Crafts and Activities for Women's Ministry
This book is packed with ideas for adding fun and creativity to women's ministry meetings and special events. Includes reproducible craft patterns, activities and more!
ISBN 08307.33671

www.family.org

The Focus on the Family Women's Series
is available where Christian books are sold.

Gospel Light
www.gospellight.com

STRENGTHEN MARRIAGES.
STRENGTHEN YOUR CHURCH.
Here's Everything You Need for a Dynamic Marriage Ministry!

Group Starter Kit includes

- Nine Bible Studies: *The Masterpiece Marriage,
  The Passionate Marriage, The Fighting Marriage,
  The Model Marriage, The Surprising Marriage,
  The Giving Marriage, The Covenant Marriage,
  The Abundant Marriage* and *The Blended Marriage*

- *The Focus on the Family Marriage Ministry Guide*

- *An Introduction to the Focus on the Family
  Marriage Series* video

Focus on the Family®
Marriage Series
Group Starter Kit
Kit Box
Bible Study/Marriage
ISBN 08307.32365

The overall health of your church is directly linked to the health of its marriages. And in
light of today's volatile pressures and changing lifestyles, your commitment to nurture
and strengthen marriages needs tangible, practical help. Now **Focus on the Family—
the acknowledged leader in Christian marriage and family resources**—gives churches
a comprehensive group study series dedicated to enriching marriages. Strengthen
marriages and strengthen your church with **The Focus on the Family Marriage Series.**